THE POWER OF COUNSELING

A Travel with My Life Gurus' and the Importance of Counseling in Schools

T.R. SRINIVASAN

Translated By
PUVIARASI THENNARASU

Notion Press

Old No. 38, New No. 6
McNichols Road, Chetpet
Chennai - 600 031

First Published by Notion Press 2018
Copyright © T.R. Srinivasan 2018
All Rights Reserved.

ISBN 978-1-64249-327-6

Dedicated

To my Father as well my friend Ramanujam, who had always granted me to carry out all my actions as per my interest and to my Mother Radha, who narrowed me at right times and showered her love in making our family perfect!

(My Father Ramanujam and My Mother Radha)

Contents

Acknowledgements

- It's my wife Tamilselvi, the reason behind writing this book. Once, when we were disputing, she challenged me to compose a book in English and then to get back to her, if at all I had to self – praise myself... She wasn't jesting, rather said it very strong. Till then I was not sure whether I would write a book on counseling. That too recollecting the memories of my amazing teachers I came across. It was nearly for a couple of weeks I was travelling through time machine that took me to my childhood and schooling arena. Though not for this book's sake, but considering this as a base, I got back my experience of how happy I was during those days, how sooner it got faded away, how beautiful the humans were in those days, how my teachers had set an example for my life... Calling back all these exhilarates me and I greatly thank my wife to make me undergo such an awesome experience...

- I thank Puviarasi foremostly, as far as this book is concerned. She held patience with all her interest in translating my Tamil writings and gripped all my suggestions in developing its English version. She is the reason for this book to get unfolded in your palms right now.

- My warm kisses to my children Adhiyaman and Amruthavarshini for letting me to pen down my experience without any commotion.

  While conversing with my son Adhiyaman, I said about this book on "School counseling" and he inquired its title. I asked him to suggest one by himself, as I had no idea that time.

  I explained him the concept of counselling on his demand.

  After listening, in less than a minute's delay he titled the book – "The Power Of Counseling…"

- I humbly dedicate my thanks to their feet of all my school teachers. Teachers are Gurus' who remain parallel to the God and this book is not without them…

- My tons of gratitude to my 'Father' Arulappan. My growth and my societal status would not have been made possible, if he wasn't there in my life as I'm nothing without him.

- I express my thanks to Raman, my nephew, who helped in spite getting rebuked by me, though did not volunteer himself, to my sister Bharathi, who ever remain as a good friend of mine in sharing all my thoughts and to my friend (Brother-in-Law) P.K.R. Muthu.

(My Wife Tamilselvi)

(My Daughter Amruthavarshini and My Son Adhiyaman)

Introduction

My thoughts sway…!
Regards to my Father, my frontmost teacher…

"Do I possess any standard or eligibility to write this book?" I questioned myself.

I studied in a way, how one must had not studied. I took decisions, one hesitated to take. I hunted for jobs in such a manner, that one had not even tried to do. It is that standard or quality I possess to write this book, I think…

I have shared my school age experiences and have narrated about my teachers who amazed me.

Also, I have expatiated about counseling, which is the prime element of this book.

I can strongly assure that this book will help and support current generation school students, their parents and teachers, with the belief that one of my Gurus Mr. Arutthanthai Arulappan who came in search of me to my place may lavish his blessings upon me.

This is not an advisory book. I do not believe in it either. This signifies a kind of counseling. Even Bhagavad Gita says that Lord Krishna, 'The First' and 'The Best' Counselor ever, rendered counseling instead of giving advice.

It's the choice of Arjuna's here either to accept or to deny.

The intention of this book is to make people understand what is counseling and career counseling, how both the terms are perceived by our society, basic psychological views on that and its introduction. I have explained things in such a way that it doesn't let down one's spirit in reading this, I think.

I wish every school to be receptive on this. Though the practice of counseling was not there during my school period, we remained mentally strong to fair extent, which is not the case with today's generation or children. Nowadays, it's only from Television or YouTube channels we hear laughter in most of the houses.

The time, the parents spend with their children have got drastically decreased and it has become uncommon for them to share their minutes with the kids nowadays. It's out of this expectation for care from the parents, children are getting departed out of their lines!

Bharadan, my nephew was studying eighth standard, when that incident happened. One evening, even after a long time, he did not return home getting down from school bus.

Everybody was in search of him hastily, confirming that he got down from the bus. But we were not able to spot where he went.

Fear started occupying everyone, speculating whether somebody would have abducted him. At last, we found him after two to three hours of search.

He had secured low marks in one of his subjects and out of fear that his parents would scold him, he started meandering without going home, post getting down from the bus. That was the reason behind his state of mind to get lost.

This mode of thinking is getting evoked within larger number of children nowadays and it's the greatest challenge for the parents to channelize these chaps!

Counseling helps dealing this kind of children and the situations at ease, for which the parents have to become more aware about this process, most importantly...
And this is my tiny step in creating such awareness!

Chapter I

Life Starts with Discipline

You can always do more than you think you can

– John Wooden

The precious and the supreme days of mine were those spent, when I was eleven to thirteen years young, that is, during my sixth to eighth standard and now, I am at my fortieth age.

Why do I feel so? Let me elaborate…

I was studying at my village's middle school till my fifth grade… (Middle school consist grade only till eighth).

My father served the same school, as an Assistant Headmaster and I was changed from my school to another school to continue from sixth standard, as my father did not want me to remain there. On an average, this happens in most of the teacher's family.

It took around four kilometres to travel to the new school in the next village, where I happened to study from sixth grade.

Before joining this school, I was warned about a person and a few things. Those were,

1. The school had a very strict and a furious headmaster
2. He had a separate cane to deal with the notorious students (it was an imported cane from his hometown). The cane had a specially designed shiny and slithery look resembling a cow's horn. But when hit with that, one can feel the shock that gets into their veins (I have experienced it once)
3. Students had to apply oil and comb their hair well
4. Students had to wear neat and tidy uniform
5. Students had to study 30 mins before the prayer starts and if anybody mutters during the study session, then he/she had to stand aside the Headmaster during the prayer and it takes a quite long time for that particular students who muttered to enter the class, as the headmaster was very stern.

Too many strict disciplinary actions and rules as these…

Whenever I heard all these regulations, my stomach started secreting excess HCL out of panic sense. At my school, I remained as a bratty one for which few scolded, few went unbothered and the rest went straight away to my father throwing complaints at my behaviour. He also had a long cane that slashed the knuckles of the students, (uh – uh, I can feel the pain even with the words) instead of slashing the palm, like other teachers…

Though I was bet for being blithe, I felt liberated at my village's school. Even now, that makes me think that it was the great freedom I had and would I get that freedom when I go to that new school?

Here, I used to be amidst my friends dissolving all my time playing around mostly and studied occasionally. Would I get all those fun going another school? Despite everything, I had a little unknown interest. So, I did not deny the offer of joining the new school. Instead, started learning cycling to commute.

Another reason for my state of interest was that, my sister had already joined the school and was continuing her studies there.

And now, I had no choice left and had to join the school for sure as per my father's opinion (He had a thought that I might get spoiled by my friends, if I had continued studying at my old school).

With thousand (not exactly!) wounds, I learnt to cycle during my fifth standard annual holidays and started cycling to the next village to continue my schooling…

Chapter 2
My First Alphabet

*Good things happen in your life when you surround
yourself with positive people*

– Roy Bennett

My hometown is Thenpalai, an hamlet located at Villupuram
district (Gingee Taluk) of Tamil Nadu, India.

Before entering the new school, let me introduce
the teachers of my village school, because they were the
rootstocks of many, during that period.

1. 'Neechathanni' Teacher
2. 'Kaivelai' Teacher
3. 'Kalathampattu' Teacher
4. 'Kannalam' Teacher
5. 'Annapallam' Teacher
6. 'Chidambaram' Teacher
7. 'Paripooranam' Teacher
8. 'Aththipattu' Teacher

My memory is working only this way. Except Paripooranam
teacher, I couldn't recall any other teachers' name and my
mind had registered merely their nicknames (original name
replaced by their place).

Out of these teachers "Neechathanni Teacher" stood
strong as my role model.

I could feel the respect for him to express my gratitude whenever I call back his name. His figure flashes my mind as fresh as the impression made on a tender tree. Thinking the way he majestically walks down my street, kindles me an "Awe" spirit even now…

He was the one who matched the word "Teacher" exactly. His way of attiring had a stylistic order! That is, undisturbed folds of starched and ironed cotton shirt with a dhoti, and a towel on his shoulder.

He was quite taller (6 feet) and always had his dhoti folded to his knees. He used to wear "Naamam" on his forehead. A Glance at him had always made me bow to his feet and get his blessing uttering "Adiyen Ramanuja!"

He had not been aggressive, but used to express a mighty speech, alike the pitch of veena strings. I did not study under him, but had noticed his way of explaining things in a very clear and précised manner which makes even a lame person to understand a concept.

As far as I perceived, I can say that all his attributes were the projection of his disciplined lifestyle.

Before I was being taught by him, he got transferred to his hometown.

I can pen all these memories that were captured by my mind between my ages of 5 to 8. Only during that time, I had seen him, but still he stands as my own legendary teacher in my thoughts and my mind can connect me quickly to his speech, action and his figure.

(I can recollect his nickname now. Yes, it's Nallaanpillaipetraal. "Nallaanpillaipetraal" was his hometown in Villupuram District, Tamilnadu).

His nickname "Neechathanni" had a reason behind it and nothing to explain much about that. He used to intake "rice water" every morning and so people around him started teasing him with that "so called" name. He least bothered those people (they all developed a syndrome sometimes later) who taunted him; because, he knew that "rice water" was the secret of his energy and health.

Chapter 3

My Learnings

*A teacher affects eternity; he can never tell where his
influence stops*

– Henry Adams

"Kaivelai" Teacher (The Term "Kaivelai" specifies self
employed). He was the one who did "Vidhyarambam"
(Hindu tradition observed on Vijayadashami day, where
children are formally introduced to learning of music,
dance, languages and other folk arts) for us. I remember him
spreading paddies and teaching us to write the first letter of
Tamil language (i.e "அ"). One had to touch his/her own
ears using hand, circling their head, to prove the teacher that
they had attained the age 5. He also did teach the children
industrial training and hence called as "kaivelai" teacher.

He used to handle subjects occasionally, when there
occurred teacher inadequacy. I hadn't shown more interest
in his classes. But, he had cordial relationships with other
students. Had seen him hitting students rarely.

Out of these teachers, 'Kalathampattu' Teacher
(Kalathampattu is a village near to mine) had a great knack
of handling subjects. He used to be louder and clearer in
his speech. If he had started taking class, it was only his

voice that remained dominative, as we had only little space between two classes unlike now.

"எண்ணென்ப ஏனை எழுத்தென்ப இவ்விரண்டும்
கண்ணென்ப வாழும் உயிர்க்கு"

**(The twain that lore of numbers and of letters give
Are eyes, the wise declare, to all on earth that live)**

(Meaning: Letters and numbers are the two eyes of a human)

The above lines are from "Thirukural" and you people would never forget this, if you had experienced his way of explaining it with all beautiful gestures… Yes, one could never forget those!

We had teachers who used to teach all the subjects despite their specialized knowledge. But they gave their best teaching in which they were familiar with.

We scored the highest in those subjects that were taught to us very clearly. The same interest encourages me to keep learning new things still.

'Kalathampattu' teacher was well versed with Tamil and Maths. Basically, he was an agriculturalist. Then, comes his teaching profession. Many a time, he had made his presence to school directly, after ploughing his field and I feel proud to register his level of dedication in his profession here.

I view his honesty and sincerity that he had shown towards agriculture and teaching as a contradiction, because these qualities which were once the normal traits of any human being, have nowadays become one's rare caliber.

These teachers were my heroes during my elementary schooling. They had never expected anything in return from us, for teaching the subjects in a way that it remains so difficult to forget even now. They gave their sincere contribution in sharing their knowledge to each and every child equally without any bias.

All these are the treasure of memories which I hold tight ever and they are registered strongly, only because they lived as the perfect examples at that time.

At this point, 'Chidambaram' Teacher (Chidambaram is a place in Cuddalore District, Tamilnadu) deserves a special mention along with a regret (i.e I did not study under him)

Once my father had fallen sick and was hospitalised due to which my mother couldn't make it to my home. So, it was 'Chidambaram' teacher who took me with him and served me idlies (South Indian food) with green chilli chutney. That was an evergreen incident stuck to my heart along with the spicy taste of green chilli chutney (I had not tasted that before in my house)

(My little mind used to ask me whether I could taste that chutney if my father fell sick once in a while…)

A very fast incident happened just before the savor of green chilli chutney faded away from my tongue. When 'Chidambaram' teacher tried boarding a train at Chidambaram railway station, he fell down in the track and got struck between the wheels of the train and oops… I was not strong enough to listen to that terrible incident when my father narrated me.

He was about thirty five years when this incident took place. He lived a humble life, but the time made his life shorter.

My father got 'Chidambaram' teacher's thought, when I'd asked him to permit me travel by train, once. He had not forgotten to ensure my safety in that case, saying, "Paathu train eru, paathupo" (Travel safely, board the train carefully)…

I still believe that 'Chidambaram' teacher is watching us both, from his paradise. Even the feel for death was taught by the teachers those days…

So, how would be the school I was about to join newly? Let me take you to that place…

Standing – From Left to Right – "Neechathanni" Teacher, "Clerk" Balaraman, "Kaivelai" Teacher and "Kalathampattu" Teacher.

Sitting – From Left to Right – Ramanujam Teacher (My Father), "Kannalam" Teacher (Head Master), I could not recollect him, "Mallandi" Teacher, "Chidambaram" Teacher, and "Athipattu" Teacher.

Chapter 4

Teachers Transform Our Lives in a Day!

There is nothing impossible to those who try

– Alexander the Great

This is a different school with different environment. Entirely unseen novel faces! Was crowded with too many teachers… Here, the school consisted of sixth to tenth standard and it's in Sevalapurai. It was about four kilometres away from my village.

First day at school… I was occupied with no fear, not nervous either… (The situation was just inverse to this when it was day 1 at my college. Even now it creates a feel of "virtual object" rolling in my abdomen. Let me explain the reason behind this later! May be in Volume II)

Lalitha Teacher!

She was my sixth standard class teacher.
A Pretty Lady…!
I basically had a thought that, "Teachers signifies old age." But she was the one who replaced my thought with "Teachers signifies beauty" too.

She dealt English class for us. A week passed by. Except her, I could not recollect anybody else teacher's name or it was like all the subjects were taught by Lalitha Teacher.

In those days, it was the class teacher who carried all the responsibilities of a class. Lack or absence of teachers had always been managed by the class teachers.

It was the month of July and the sun was spiting heat rays across our village.

The only thing I disliked about my new school was saline water. I understood later that it was not only the problem at school but the problem of whole village. Except a pond, it was saline water that was available almost everywhere …

Because of this, during class intervals, that particular pond used to overflow with heads consuming the non saline water!

It was after such an interval, the English class commenced. The memories are still fresh in my mind. The sand sheet where we sat and listened our subjects… Weaved thatch, the class wall made of mud supported by a coconut trunk…

Lalitha Teacher had the habit of making children read out loud, the previous day's lesson line by line. It's because, English had never been our favourite or acceptable language. Somehow, a week passed by. But I got caught that particular day!

Everyone was reading that particular lesson (For a very long period that was in my memory, but not now) paragraph by paragraph. Few tried reading it to some extent. Few were really making their best in reading. Few ceased very soon, as fast as how they started. They were not able to read. Teacher neither said a word nor berated them. She just asked them to meet her in person later. That's it!

It was my turn then. I took the book in my hand. Gazed at the paragraph that I was supposed to read.. I could not read. I was unsure how to scan it. I did not even make an effort on that. Teacher was watching me.

"What's your name?"

"Seenuvasan"(By that time I had not become 'Srinivasan')

"To Dress well is alone not enough. It's important to study well too. Tomorrow it's your turn to read out the whole lesson" – Teacher was not angry and did not cane me as well. But she was very polite yet strict in conveying that to me. Other than that, I was not told a word by her rest of the day.

I must say you about the "dress," that she chose to address me when I stood reading nothing.

That was a very swanky T – Shirt. The buttons on that was not made out of ordinary plastic… Those were gleamy like stainless steel. The shirt had a very short sleeve and many floral designs at the front. During 1988 its price was Rs. 70/-. It was quite a large amount for my family during those days.

That was the time when "Readymade" dresses started occupying the market. It was purchased at Haneefa Textile at Pondy Bazaar located in T. Nagar, Chennai. It was only then

I realised the conjuration of advertisements and Haneefa was very famous that time.

My father bought me that dress by getting entranced with the beaut of it. It was such a historically extolled T-shirt that embarrassed me in front of Lalitha teacher. Earlier to me, it was my father who was abashed by my mother for buying that shirt offering such a high price. It's due its lustrousness, people were jealous to buy it.

I least bothered the teacher when she criticized the beauty of my learning, but it was the moment when she knocked at my dress I got wild… "Did she know amid how much difficulty I got that dress?" My thought was whirling only around that…

Only after reaching home, it banged my mind that I have got English as my first class the next day. I was quite; spoke nothing with nobody at home. I did not utter a word even to my sister when cycled back from school…

I sat down opening the English volume and my father was relaxing on his easy chair that evening!

My father disfavoured the practice of parents learning subjects, music, silambam etc., for their children's sake. Though he was a teacher, he had not taught a word for my sister and me.

After a short hesitation, recited him the story of how I stood staring without reading the English lesson at school. He said this, looking me up and down. "Read the way how you read Tamil, just by joining the letters and if at all you get struck with any unknown words, ask me… I'll help you. But I won't learn for you nor teach you line by line"

As far as I remember, that was the first and the very last time, when I asked him subject related queries. I then determined to do anything that comes my way on my own. It should be I, who has to decide everything.

I read that lesson at least 50 times. I encouraged myself and it gave birth to my confidence, "The next day I must be the Hero and from that day I should continue to be the same!"

I became one of the favourite students of Lalitha Teacher from the very next day. She introduced me to all her colleagues. Within six months everybody started recognizing me and before the end of the year I became so familiar. From that day till the date I left the school, the badge "First rank student" remained as one of my possessions.

Note:

It was a month after, when Lalitha teacher said about my dress, we got the pattern of dressing uniform in schools. Before that, schools had a rule of wearing uniform only once in a week.

Just because of that rule, I got escaped from others getting envious upon me for wearing pretty dresses!

Chapter 5

'Reflection' is the HEART of Teaching!

Attitude is a little thing that makes a big difference

– Winston Churchill

'Melacheri' Krishnan Teacher (Melachery is a place near Sevalpurai) – The unique and an exceptional teacher. Initially I wasn't showing interest in his class thinking that he explained affairs out of the subject. It was during my eighth standard I realized that I had mistook his teaching

When handling history, he used to narrate all the matters that were related to an incident. For instance, if subject says about Ibrahim Lodi, in an hour he explains the whole story about him. Not in usual way, but had given us a feel of watching a full length movie. With up and down pitches, like a story said by a father to his kid, with all his face gestures with a sudden suspense…and after a long delay he breaks that. His class was the fusion of anger, surprise, humanity, murder… Just like reading a beautiful novel!

One would start loving history, if had heard his story of narrating on how many time Muhammad bin Tughluq played changing his capital…

I remember him neither speaking an extra word other than the subject nor appreciating anybody for getting high marks or scolding for securing low marks. One thing to insist about him is that, he used to express his opinions like a friend.

His belief – "Our students should learn well, grasping everything with utmost interest and they knew what to do next…"

Once, when I was reading Madhan's "Vanthargal Venrargal," it was Melacheri teacher's thought that darted my mind. We'd got such an energy and spirit through his class.

Sahaya Mary Teacher – We were almost like friends. She took science during my 8th standard.

Just 10 mins was enough for her, to picturise any diagram (bisection of a flower or a flat bottomed flask, whatever) on the blackboard. Within couple of minutes she used to colour it too lovely.

Later her details on that diagram and the way she places example used to be in right proportion. I had not experienced her being late to the class or leaving the class late. Very well versed in time management.

A mirthful teacher… Affectionate one, at the same time if she had found anybody mumbling in the class, they wouldn't escape from her lash. But, had the habit of apologizing from Jesus later, saying "Yesappa" (Jesus), for slashing them!

The annual day event had always made Sagaya Mary teacher very energetic that kept her busy most of the time… She used to teach music and dance for the selected students. She had sung her own composition too.

Whenever I hear the song "Vellichalangaihal konda kalaimagal" (Ilayaraja's composition from the movie "Kaadhal Oviyam"), the girl who danced for it and the Sahaya Mary teacher who choreographed it strike my mind.

She made one of my friends to dance for "Aadungal paadungal pillai ponvandugal," a song from the movie "Guru" (Ilayaraja's composition). From then, my friend became the school's hero. I guess, I was dancing too, somewhere in the stage's corner for that song…

She remained as a great coordinator ensuring, that everything goes perfect during the annual day by listing the events orderly with no confusions. She imparted us Human Resource Management without teaching literally.

No matter what sort of work I carry out, I do it with my farthest interest, perfection, sincerity and with proper planning. All these are the traits that were acquired by me or by us from our teachers!

It's them who fed our roots (Our daily activities) with water, removed our weeds and made our base strongly fix into this world.

Whenever we credited Sahaya Mary teacher with these words, she used to move away with a smile, gently. Still she remains the same!

Chapter 6
The REAL Master!

*"Discipline is helping a child solve a Problem.
Punishment is making a child suffer for having a
problem. To raise problem solvers,
focus on solution not retribution."*

– L.R. Knost

S. Senthil Perumal (Su. Senthir Perumal, to write in Tamil) – It is the name that shook and terrified us during our school days. It's him, whom we had a glimpse about, in chapter one, Our Headmaster… Not only in Gingee, but in the whole district of Villupuram, it was Sevalapurai High School that stood, "The best" in maintaining utmost discipline and high pass percentage in those days.

All these were made possible by S. Senthil Perumal Headmaster through dignity and control over his school and that was a history and a village chapter as well. Kanyakumari is his hometown. Yearly once he used to visit his place and rest of the days here.

I can feel the smell of "Javadhu" (Javadhu Powder made out of Javadhutree) along with fragrance of "Vibhuthi" (ash made out of dried burnt wood) around me, when I just say his name. Neatly combed hair, his long pant with full sleeve shirt… It was majestic seeing him!

An unfaltering! He had that pride of being a teacher! Seeing him at once makes us to stand. Other teachers held such a respect for him…

Respect was taught us through their living in those days!

I was studying sixth and my sister was at her 9th standard, my memory says… One day, during the class hour, I noticed my sister standing in front of my class speaking with our teacher. She then approached me straight away saying, "Headmaster koopidraru. Enga classku vaa" (Headmaster is calling you. Come to my class). I wasn't able to figure out for what he called me. I did not panic. However, he was S. Senthil Perumal, right? So had a little fear!

My sister did not say anything more. I just followed her and wished him entering the class. He accepted and made me stand in front of the blackboard. Few seconds later, he asked me to take a chalk.

"Inga nikraangailla, intha moonu annangalukum nee oru moonu vaarthai English – il solli kkodakanum, sariya?" (Teach three english words to all these three brothers standing here. Okay?), he asked me.

I got scared more now. But, did not expose my fear, as Lalitha Teacher flashed my mind.

This is what he asked.
What is 'he?'
What is 'she?'
What is 'it?'
I remained quite…

"Unaku ithu theriyuma?" (Do you know this?), he asked. "Theriyum" (I know) I said.

"Thamizh la athuku artham ezhuthu" (Write the tamil meaning of these words), he added!

"Avan,

Aval,

Athu," I wrote and looked at him.

He questioned those three. "Ithukooda ungaluku theriyalai. Paaru, ungalaivida moonu varusham chinnapaiyan" (Even this you students do not know? But look at this boy who is three years younger to you!) Stating this, he turned to me saying "moonu per mandaiyilum ongi orukottuvai" (knock all the three on their head)

I felt embarrassed. Initially I knocked them very slowly. But he asked me to do it hard and then, I made my best. Those brothers encouraged me either and whispered in my ears, "Paravailla, ongikotitidu, illaina pirambadi. Athuku ithuve thevalam" (It's okay, knock hardly, or else he may beat us with cane and for that getting knocked is better). I understood.

When got introduced to him proudly on that day, I did not guess that a big insult was waiting for me by him (Headmaster) in my 7th standard.

Those days, we used to create a lot of our own games. One among those was, making others to predict about the actor or actress whom we thought of.

We need to conceive a number, through which a question would be asked. The answer for that had to be linked with another question which relates to an actor or actress exactly and it was my favourite game.

One fine day, in the absence of our teacher, I started playing that particular game and the HM who crossed our class noticed us performing it!

Everybody was treated well, for playing that game in the class.

He looked up me, when it was my turn to get the reward. "Intha vilayaatu vilayadathaan avlo thooram cycle la variya? Unga appakita sollava?" (Just to play this, are you travelling to school from your place? Should I say this to your father?) he asked me and slashed twice with that imported cane…

I did not play any game after that. Not only in school, but in college too… Nowhere I had played the game after that!

"Ozhukam Uyirinum Ombapadum!"
("Decorum to be preserved carefully more than the life!")

Chapter 7

School Subjects Vs Life Subjects

Tell me and I will forget. Show me and I may remember. Involve me and I learn

– Benjamin Franklin

The teachers of this school played an important role, to set myself a few disciplinary rules in life. Our teachers, through their living, taught us how crucial the self discipline remains in one's life and they even passed those values to their next generation at ease.

These school teachers explained us, that life subjects are more significant than those of school subjects with perfect examples. What's failure, how it pains, how to handle it, how to admire the success, how to accept challenges, the importance of sports, being friendly, sharing food, difference between competition and jealousy… Altogether, they all developed humanity and they brought up us as humans!

Not only these… Every teacher taught us that subjects should be learnt only by understanding the concept and not by memorizing. The same habit continued within me.

But that was obstructed for a short period in my next school or it was the environment which I disliked and made me struggle…

Chapter 8
Saint's Visit to My Place

No matter the problem, kindness is always the right response

– L.R. Knost

Arutthanthai Arulappan! (Arutthanthai denotes Reverend Father)

Principal of Punitha Annal Melnilai palli (St. Ann's Higher Secondary School), Tindivanam.

It was during my school period itself; the school had completed its centenary.

He had a unique identity and was more furious than S. Senthil Perumal Headmaster. His cane was also an imported one. I couldn't detect from where it got imported, till date!

It's an unparalleled beauty to look at the way, he used to walk around that "U" shaped school premises in his white "Angi" (An attire). I hadn't seen him rambling doing nothing with his cane but just orbiting it gently. He used to strike the students with that rolling cane, crossing him, softly. Cane played only on those who were very mischievous. Apart from that, it remained as his object of confidence.

I completed my eighth and was awaiting the entrance exam result to join in St. Ann's., Tindivanam.

It had been a great entertainment for us to jump and swim in the well during our summer vacation in my village.

It was during such a day; Arutthanthai Arulappan sir visited our house. Since, it was a very famous school in Tindivanam those days; Mr. Arulappan was used to the influence of great parties that pressured him. Though, only on the basis of eligibility (good score) he had given admission for the students in his school. Moreover, he was very particular in admitting the students with only good marks especially for sixth and ninth grade.

Due to this hectic process, post making "Admission list" he used to leave Tindivanam and travelled to nearby places on his two wheeler for relaxation…

It was during that kind of travel, he stopped by our house that was on his way. My father knew Mr. Arulappan well and had a pure respect for him as he was a teacher too. That bond made him to reach our house after a short search…

I was busy playing "Ori" inside the Well that time. ('Ori' is a game played inside the Well). A person was sent to call me and it was my sister. "Tindivanam school Headmaster vanthirkaaru. Unnai paakanumnu sonaaru" (Tindivanam school Headmaster has come to see you), my sister conveyed.

As soon as I entered my home, I was confused about how to call him seeing his attire. He sighted me fondly, who appeared before him with dripping dress…

Understanding my hesitation, "Poi dress change pannituvaa" (Get your dress changed), he said me.

Minutes later, I stood in front him after changing my cloth.

"Unaku intha varusham admission potaachu. Ithaivida nalla padikanum, sariya?" (You have got admission this year. You must read well than now. right?) He asked.

(My father already tried joining me sixth standard in that school. But it went in vain, as I did not clear the entrance test)

"Sari" (Okay) I said. I wasn't even cautious to "Thank" him for offering me the admission.

After a general talk with my father Mr. Arutthanthai Arulappan departed...

I get horripilated recollecting those moments, when such a "Saint" came in search of my place to catch a very normal fellow like me!

It was a blessing! A blessing from my Guru... Have no more words to say!

Yes, he was a "Saint" and it's not an ordinary word. His life was very pure just like his white uniform that he wore. It was the life of a sage that resembled a tidy stream!

Everybody called him "Saamiyar" (Sage) and he lived a life that reflected the exact meaning of it. He remained as a perfect example for his religion. He led a very simple life and used to express his views shortly.

Without him my four years of studies wouldn't had been possible. Even after that, he travels with me without my knowledge. Yes, my mind and noes is drum everything late.

By the time, when I was in a completely "raised up" position and was about to thank my "Guru," he had left this world. I realized his grandness, only during his absence.

He had been my reason of everything. Almost, he was the one who had continuously fed water for my growth!

From ninth to twelfth standard, I studied staying in hostel. It was a "Golden Jubilee" hostel and was run by St. Ann's Higher Secondary School itself. The fee they had charged was Rs. 250/-. When I was studying twelfth, the fee was doubled. It was a normal expense and a very normal fee.

Everything was fair. But my nature did not allow me to adjust with the hostel environment.

I hated it and that four years of life brought me up with least knowledge about the world!

Rev. Father A. Arulappan (Picture taken in
the year 1994)

Chapter 9

Did I Need Freedom or Protection?

The only disability in life is a bad attitude

– Scott Hamilton

If I'm being raised a question whether it is the "Freedom" or the "Protection" that an individual requires, I would strongly prefer 'Freedom' in that case. It's merely the freedom that makes a person complete. Being inside the web of protection, one can't speak…no! One cannot even think about freedom.

My freedom was grabbed in this hostel. I was raised in a village and without seeing my people, I wasn't able to pass a day. Be it the cows, the goats, the farm and fields, the wells, the lakes… I was not separated from these till my eighth standard. There were no place left, I spent my days playing, running here and there. All were friends. All were relatives. All became foes too, when it happened to be a fight.

Except home work I hadn't learnt any other school subjects at home. Just listening keen to the subjects during the class was enough for me and used to go through the subject before the exam. That's it. Studies hadn't burdened me anytime, as I approached learning with a feel of liberty and I was allowed to do that. I made my best too. Also, I'd participated in competitions. Participation itself made me proud where winning was secondary.

I had the confidence of facing any kind of situation. I hadn't pulled myself back to express my views on anything. Either victory or failure, I was in the state of accepting it equally and my life was pleasant!

But, from the day when I joined the hostel, nothing was at my ease. The days, I hadn't cried were very less. Gradually, I got used to it. Those tears weekend me. A kind of fear got stuck with me. I curbed myself. I neither questioned nor answered my situation. I was just one among the others. Didn't yield either a bad name or achieved anything great...

Hostel indicated the way of living a scheduled life. Had to know everything seeing at the notice board everyday... Within a month, my physique and mind got adapted to that scheduled life.

According to that, one had to wake up at 5.15 a.m and we were practiced to exercise 20 minutes after brushing. Before 6 a.m we had to bath and assemble at the "Study Hall." There was no rule that students had to necessarily empty their bowel only in the morning. In those days whenever you were getting time or getting a place you can get it done. In my four years of schooling, I can count the days, when I got it emptied, during morning time.

We were almost about three hundred to three fifty students and what would be the condition of just six or seven lavatories if all of us had tried to empty out our bowels only by morning?

Tindivanam persisted as a land of saline water. Pure water was made available only for drinking purpose which got distributed through Motor trucks. I had only saline water bathing in these four years. For me it's just four years, while few experienced it for seven years!

I detested the saline water bathing to an extreme. The thing that I liked there the most, was the evening sports we played. Volleyball, Football, Basketball… I loved playing all the three. Sometimes, Father had also played with us. The mandatory information that I got, as soon as I joined the school was that, Mr. Arutthanthai Arulappan must only be called as "Father."

"One – day gardening," was a definite task. Father used to barber someone's hair every evening. During my four years of study I remember being barbered by him four, five times. It was during those times father used to get transformed into a kid. "Whatever work to be done, it has to be carried out with one's utmost interest" – This was his policy. It may be barbering, cleaning toilets, gardening or to serve food at the dining hall… He expected things to be done perfectly. He did not want anybody to speak during ingestion…

Those who escaped for cinema shows at night were made to kneel down two to three days out of their respective classrooms by him. I have heard that our previous batch students who involved in such acts were given TC (Transfer Certificate) and sent out from the school.

Students who did the same during my period were forgiven by Father. Likewise, Father was the major reason for my aversion (got developed when I joined this school) to get dumped within me eventually…

Within the next one and half month, we got our monthly test over and the rank cards were handed out by Father. My science score was "34" in that test. "Puthu idam. Puthu teacher, hostel…ethu venaalum kaaranama irukum. Aduthamurai naan unnai ipdi paaka kudaathu. Po" (New place, new teachers and hostel…reason might be anything. But I should not see you scoring like this anymore…) Except this, he said me nothing. As per hostel's practice, defaulters used to get two cane slashes for sure. But that did not happen as Father had confidence over me and I can say proudly that I kept his confidence up, till I finished my schooling…

Chapter 10

Marks – The Only Intention

Education's purpose is to replace empty mind with an open one

– Malcolm Forbes

It's solely our Father's memories that invade my mind, when I retrieve my hostel days. Apart from him, nobody's authority kept me closest… Mr. Arulappan teacher was such an honest, truthful and a selfless saint who led a respectable and a lovely life. This kind of humans will appear occasionally as God's Messengers…my belief believes strongly!

Yet, Let me draft a short note on the teachers whom I'd admired and astonished looking at!

Vanathaiyan Teacher

He hadn't handled any subjects for us and I was not known to him. Still, he remained as one of the Tamil teachers whom I had amazed at… Sweet was his Tamil, great poet and a peachy orator as well. Every annual day had at least one of his handworks!

Not only for him, but except Father I wasn't known to anybody else in that school. It's because I did not do anything for my recognition nor feltlike doing anything great. Totally, I did not have a chance to get into that state of mind.

Nagarajan Teacher

I scored 92 marks in science during my 10th public exam and it was the same mark which I said that I would get, at my home. The reason behind it was Nagarajan sir. He had always delivered more clarity in his teaching and was strict equally. Just teaching had not been his habit. He used to keep explaining the subject until everybody captures the concepts as he expected.

Marks were his only intention and he achieved it brilliantly making students to obtain high scores as per our education system. Nobody could blame him in that case.

I flunked initially, as I wasn't interested in memorizing the subjects line by line... Later, I was very sure about not letting down Father's confidence on me and started adapting to that.

Moreover, till tenth standard, subjects weren't that difficult to learn...

Nagarajan sir had his own set of protocols. He used to bath twice a day (within the school timing). Morning once and after lunch once, only after bathing he'd entered the school. Morning a shirt and by noon, another shirt... The aroma of the beetle slices and Javadu always lingered around him. His forehead used to bear vibhuthie'er. Very dynamic person... I had not seen him taking class sitting in his chair. To add, he had not carried the book in his hands, instead got it stacked in his brain!

Also, his house entrance had always been over flooded with the students. He was very famous during those days, for which he conducted separate tuition classes...

My wonder for tuitions started from there. Because, I had a thought that special classes were only meant for the students those who were in need of special attention. But my guess was completely proved wrong after landing at Tindivanam...

Mariyanantham Teacher

He was quite opposite to Nagarajan Teacher. A jovial person… He handled English for us. It was his habit to share everything with his students. Since, it was boys' school; most of his gags were of typically "Adults type."

Examples that he quoted other than subject matters are still kept safe by me. He had the knack of imparting good thoughts to us via subjects. I think, it was from him, I started understanding the term "Counseling."

Its lot of Mariyanantham teachers our schools require nowadays, to meet the emergency of the students in expressing their thoughts and opinions to anyone, with no difficulties.

For that, he hadn't used obscene words at any cost. His jokes were very familiar, as those did not lead the students in the wrong path. Most of the students used to xerox him, through their words.

It was only Mariyanantham teacher's class that had been like a festival. At the same time; he had not failed to strict us if we were wrong!

Well-nigh, he used to cover all the stuffs that matters to lead a meaningful life, in an hour's class and he did that continuously. This is the point where he stood unique.

He tried to make us believe, his level best, directly or indirectly, that it was only out of the subjects our life lays. It is an undeniable truth that I did not come across any such legendary teachers, later at any time in my life…

Chapter II

Life Coach

Do not go where the path may lead; go instead where there is no path and leave a trail

– Ralph Waldo Emerson

Father suggested me to learn through English medium after my tenth standard. At the beginning, I struggled, but later, managed the language…

Still, it was then and now, English always had stayed and will stay as only a secondary language to me. Because it's in Tamil, I can generate my thoughts, foremostly. That habit will never change. Joining college and then joining at a job, everything happened only through this experience… I may need a separate chapter (or book) to describe that long journey, that involves me, speaking amid crowd or in a team with no diffidence!

I'm cerebrating now. Father would have left me to decide my language. But he did not do that. He strongly believed that we need a second language to learn and he expected a change to happen for us, in future. It's not only for me he proposed that, but for many other students alike me.

He was not just a "Father," but also persisted as a very good "Life coach" for us.

That noble man's thought was exactly right and still continues to be right! I realised the importance of English language when I started hunting for a job!

Chapter 12
My Unturned Aspirations!

It always seems impossible until it is done

– Nelson Mandela

I did not go through life's learning process greatly, during my eleventh and twelfth standard…

I neither experienced things that revolted my mind nor developed an interest on anything. Alike most students, during those days (even now) I had the same aspiration or had a fake thought that it was my desire (not my inner conscious one)

That was, studying medicine, post twelfth!

Before that…!

I have already shared right? The hostel remained as a solitary place for me after joining it…and till exiting it, my feel hadn't switched. The more I enjoyed my village life like a free bird, the more I suffered like a caged bird that had got its limbs tied, in those four years…

I got my thinking depleted and my action had lost his potential completely. I had no confidence. The reasons behind these were:

1. I wandered in my village with all my autonomy. I studied more and played equally more with my friends listening songs and radio, reading comics etc…nothing out of these, I had at my hostel, except studies.

2. I had no friends at all. Excluding few, most of the students were from small or big cities. I disliked their habits completely or it was my habit that they disdained.

3. It had been studies, only studies occupied with silence, only silence…and that silence did not let me sleep. No amusements at all. Because of that, I became dazed. Few were used to it and I pretended that I got used to it too…

4. It was during my eighth standard itself, I was very clear that scoring mark was different and getting succeeded in life was different. But this hostel life had puzzled me a little. I stayed muddy…

5. There was no connection with the outer world. No human's odour I felt. I had no idea about acquitting with people.

6. My General knowledge was at "Zero" level. I was unaware about aptitude; attitude as these weren't taught to us.

7. I attempted my subjects, by understanding the concepts, till my eighth grade. But it was when I started memorizing the subjects; my confidence started losing its marks. Our education system expects us to replicate each and every line exactly from the text books onto the test paper during the exams. With those confusions, I, who memorized the subjects, scored marks in my exams, but lost the power of understanding the meaning of it.

Basically, I was quite contrary to this!

Chapter 13

Sense of Interest

If a child can't learn the way we teach, maybe we should teach the way they learn

Tamil Teacher

I disremembered to cite about my Tamil teacher. He taught us Tamil during my eighth standard in Sevalapurai and was called fondly as "Ayya" by us. He was the owner of mellifluous voice and spellbound Tamil pronunciation. We might have come across people who sing flawlessly. But, he was the one who used to speak flawlessly. He had a twisted moustache and had always used to wear white shirt with dhoti and coloured shirts occasionally.

He was an admirer of arts. At times he used to make us sing where he had also joined us. I still remember the song that I sung during my turn and it was "Kaathirunthu kaathirunthu kaalangal poguthadi," an entire song from "Vaithegi kaathirunthaal" (Ilayaraja's composition)

"It's not the voice or tone that's important to sing but just to make an attempt itself is appreciable," he used to boost us. He encouraged us to adore everything, even to eat up with interest. I felt too fresh and different hearing him. I used to consume food as if it was my responsibility.

Later, I implemented my Tamil Ayya's technique and I liked doing that.

He was the one who strongly sowed me with "sense of interest." After that I started working out all my duties with my utmost involvement. This "sense of interest" got completely parted away from me after entering Tindivanam's hostel or I did find no such teachers to impart such kind of feel within me. Even a **"Perpetual lamp"** needs someone to light up it. Right?

Chapter 14
Why Did I Need Counseling?

When you reach the end of your rope, Tie a knot in it and hang on it

– Thomas Jefferson

Later, joining Tindivanam hostel, the thing which I regretted the most or my habit which I felt like prohibited was reading books…

Because, it was from sixth standard I had started reading comics. Comics, how many imaginative forts would have I built? I can write or discuss that separately, as I have got a lot to say about those memories.

During summer vacations my sister and I, along with few friends of mine used to read comics and had exchanged reading story books.

We had a sequence of reading comics first and then the novels published in "Rani Muthu" (A Tamil magazine). Later, the thriller novels… I did not have interest on thriller stories and "Ambuli mama" was my favourite. Vedhalam, Vikramathithan stories from those impressed me a lot. The one which affected me the more was "Mithilavilas" by the writer Lakshmi published in "Rani Muthu" Magazine.

I used to read daily, weekly (Vikatan, Kumutham) and monthly magazines.

The day when I joined Tindivanam's hostel, I lost everything. A complete four years…and I hadn't read even a book. During my twelfth I was presented Kannadasan's "Manampolavazhvu" ("Life as one desire"), a book and how many times to read that same book again and again?

My brain went numb reading the same subject books again and again. I missed my tendency of conceiving anything new and fresh. It was only subjects that occupied us, right from waking up in the morning till going to the bed at night.

In the hostel, except subject books no other materials were allowed to read and the hostel warden used to throw his sharp sight on us every now and then. Nobody knew when and who would get caught by him. Hence, I hadn't tried to hide and read those non-subject books.

These ways, though the wings of a free bird were cut down, it did its duty of studying and scored marks.

There was no difference between the parrot being with the "Parrot Astrologer" and me. Paddy grains used to be spread as soon the bird's cage gets opened and for that the parrot had to pick a card from the shuffled pack. It enters back into its cage after picking the card and this is what its daily task. And the parrot forgets its propensity of flying eventually!

As days' passes, it will be a big question for itself whether it's a bird! It doesn't know his nature, its strengths and weaknesses. Similarly, it will be the others in our life who decide what we need to do. And I think it's here, I must detail about the process of "Counseling" and "Career Counseling"

Chapter 15
Purpose of This Book

Whether you believe you can, or believe you can't, you are usually right

– Henry Ford

This is not an autobiography that I have written to narrate myself. Moreover, I haven't achieved anything great to compose an auto biograph. The utmost intention of these pages were, If I had got counseled on my career at the right time, I would had not studied Engineering which was totally irrelevant to my interest or if I had known something about that in advance, I would have self analyzed myself not to choose that.

We all have just a life and will it be signified if lived for others sake? Maybe, we can earn money, but can one yield their liberty of joy and happiness out of that?

Who am I? What's possible for me? What are my endowments? What are the courses and job choices that fit my interests? What should I do to pursue my job with the sense of satisfaction and joy?

Won't many achievements' cross our way if we involve ourselves running behind our passion with overall interest, care and eagerness?

Winners are so…right? They sacrifice themselves completely to achieve what they desire at and it's possible for them, only because they have identified who they are…

Scoring marks merely and carrying out the course by just believing or listening to someone else opinions and joining a job and after a certain point, letting everything to become "something" may erode once career. The same happened for me. My interest was on arts and science, literature and psychology related courses. And I would have given my cent percent involvement in these. I would have not forgotten things easily and nothing would have been difficult to understand. It would have led to the inception of new questions. I would have worked effortlessly to find solutions for my queries.

Under science, physics was my favourite subject and then botany. It was the chapter, "Sound" that I liked the most in physics. I would have chosen "Sound engineering" for my interest. But I wasn't aware about that during those days.

I can never blame my father when it comes to my education. Because it was the freedom he gave us, concerns me in that case. Till date he hasn't interfered in our interests. That too, post my college days he had no opinions to stop or restrict us.

The purpose of this book is to exhibit my initial stages of school life, how I faced my important phase of eleventh and twelfth standard, my learning from those days and from the teachers, how I struggled in choosing my college and course and how it affected me. It also portrays my relationship with the teachers whom I had come across and the understandings about them that led to changes in my life, their personal traits those amazed and impacted me.

Very importantly, it explains my phase from first standard to twelfth standard and my life before and after hostel days. With the belief that, discussion about these and my research on self analysis and self understanding may benefit many other students, I have started penning this…

I will elaborate what happened next, after my schooling, college, job search and the rest in the forthcoming days, through a separate volume.

It's the school days for maximum number of students where their future lies in. If their schooling period supports strong enough by incorporating them with required knowledge, then the rest would fall in places to fair extent for major of the students.

And for that every school has to promote "Counseling" and the "Counselors" are most important for that to happen. Now, let me discuss the relationship between these two words.

Chapter 16
Misconceptions of Counseling

*If you want children to keep their feet on the ground,
put some responsibility on their shoulders*

– Abigail Van Buren

Here, the word counseling is perceived with misconception and the most critical misconceptions are shared below,

1. "Counseling" is given for only those who are mentally challenged or given only for the children who are in need of special attention.

2. "Career Counseling" is defined as just referring the students on choosing specific college or courses advertising that "This college or this course is the best" or "This college has earned cent percentage in placements" and asking the students to join the referred college blindfoldedly.

"Counseling" and "Career Counseling" are brilliant terms which have been misunderstood as per one's convenience or have been taught us in the same way mostly...

Because of these when a counselor approaches the parents regarding counseling, their immediate reply is "why is that for my child? He or she is perfectly doing well!"

Career Counseling is really all about,

1. Suggesting your children, the field or course of study that fits their interest based on their natural ability or traits and their level of involvement.
2. Conducting a series of discussion with your child to analyse their thought process and to identify their alternate plans if they have any, in achieving their goals.
3. Determining whether the child is heading towards the right direction or yet to find his/her path, after a discussion with them and a research followed by it.
4. Making them conscious about what stream to choose after tenth and how to prepare themselves to choose their desired course of study.
5. Identifying your children's strengths and weaknesses.
6. Assisting the children to overcome their state of instability. For instance, few might be interested in science, but they avoid investing time to learn or focus. In that case proper counseling can enhance their focus or concentration level.
7. Guiding students who are interested in joining ITI (Industrial Training Institute) after High School. Based on their ability, the counselor explains how to choose their domain and make them know the job opportunities in that particular field.
8. Leading the students who wish to move abroad for their graduations after twelfth and also provides them the particulars about the universities that offer their desired courses and make them clear on how to prepare for the relevant entrance exams.
9. Facilitating the parents to guide their children on decision making as it's not only their child's future

that's involved but also involves the investment made by the parents on their children. Based on this aspect, both the children and the parentswill be suggested to make out the best decision on choosing one's higher studies or career.

Each and every child in unique and so, a single solution or suggestion cannot match or solve every one's confusions. Hence, it's very crucial for the children and the parents to have a guide to travel with them for a short or a long term based on their need and that guide who can trip with them is a "Career Counselor"

It's highly impossible to balance the thoughts of children with that of the elder ones.' Hence, each and every individual requires different process or procedures to be followed or prescribed.

For an instance, Sugarcane cannot be processed in a single step and it has to undergo series of procedures to get converted into sweet sugar grains. Similarly, whenever a child or a student completes his or her academic, they need series of counseling to take place to overcome their difficulties at every phase that helps to foresee a fruitful future for them.

Children's thoughts and intentions keep changing so rapidly and it's not necessary for them to follow usual path alike others. They can be taught, corrected and suggested to reach their unique goals. They can also be enabled to foresee the consequences and impacts about their chosen path in achieving their dreams.

On the other hand, most of the parents drive their children to satisfy their needs and aspirations, and that's totally unfair to make children follow their parent's dreams or make them to get into something which they aren't interested in, as that will end up buying the depression for their children by parents themselves.

One can doubt, why I narrated about my teachers and school life initially, in this context of counseling. There's lies a very strong reason behind it and before dealing with that, it's my responsibility here to share the truth or to introduce the awareness about **"Career Counseling."**

Chapter 17

The History of Counseling

When a person is devoted to something with complete faith, I unify his faith in that. Then, when his faith his completely unified, he gains the object of his devotion

– Bhagavad Gita

"Career Counseling" originated in the United States, in the later of 19th century out of societal convulsion, transition, and change. This was described by historians as a progressive social reform movement aimed at eradicating poverty and substandard living conditions that had been created by the rapid industrialization and consequent migration of people to major urban centres' at the turn of the 20th century.

Stages of Career Counseling

First Stage: Job Placement Services (1890–1919)

The focus of the first stage in the history of career counseling was job placement. Frank Parsons, the founder of career counseling, established a settlement house program for young people already employed or currently unemployed, who had been displaced during this period of rapid change. The placement of these young people into new jobs was one of the initial and most important purposes of this new agency.

Parson's career counseling model was grounded in simple logic and common sense and relied on the observing and interviewing skills of the counselor. He stated that there are three broad factors in the choice of an occupation: (1) knowledge of self, (2) knowledge of the requirements for success in different occupations, (3) matching these two groups of facts.

Psychological testing, an important factor is the first functional stage in career counseling, that is, self-assessment.

Second Stage: Educational Guidance in the Schools (1920–1939)

Educational counseling, the second stage in the development of career counseling emerged from the work of humanitarian, progressive social reformers in the schools to promote the career development in order to match the increased needs for literacy, to cope with the increasing demands of industrialization and to increase the number of school-going children.

Third Stage: Colleges and Universities and the Training of Counselors (1940–1959)

The new social transition after World War I was engendered by two major events: World War II and the USSR's (Union of Soviet Socialist Republics)

These two social conditions led to the rise of the professional practice of career counseling: (1) the personal and career problems of veterans, especially those who were disabled during the war; (2) the influx of new types of students to higher education (generally older, non-traditional)

Fourth Stage: Meaningful Work and Organizational Career Development (1960–1979)

The 1960's were the time of idealism, hope and at the beginning of it; the unemployment rate was 8.1%, the highest since the 1930s in US. President Kennedy after entering office in 1961, appointed a panel of consultants on vocational education who issued their report, which stated that school counselors need to also have exceptional understanding of the world of work and its complexities.

Many young people wanted meaningful jobs that would allow them to change the world for the better. The United States was regarded as a rich, sophisticated, yet humane nation and young people wanted the United States to live up to its ideals. Career information was to have far-reaching consequences in the next 20 years from then, to supply the information needs to the career counselors who required such data for their livelihood and to the general public who required such data for career decision making.

Fifth Stage: Independent Practice of Career Counseling and Outplacement Counseling (1980–1989)

The late 1970's, however, were characterized by a declining economic system rather by the growth and prosperity of the early 1960's. This began with the transition of industrial age to the age of information & technology and that led to loss of jobs in the industrial sectors of US economy, increased demands of employers for technological skills, loss of permanent jobs to contract labour and loss of job security.

During this stage, the national acceptance of career counseling took place and it provided occupational transition along with proliferation of mental health practices. This resulted in the expansion and growth of the professional practice of career counseling extensively.

Sixth Stage: New Directions (1990–Present)

At the end of the 1980's and at the beginning of the 1990's, career counseling found itself being extended in a variety of new directions: upward (outplacement, senior executives, with attorneys), downward (poor people, resume writers for homeless), outward (schools and agencies through federal legislation), and inward (multicultural and other specialties).

The ***upward extension*** was into the populations of business executives who had found looking for work, at times, in their lives after planning for a financially successful retirement from the companies that they had spent their entire lives building.

The ***downward extension*** was into the poor and homeless socioeconomic classes who were being required to work because of new governmental policies. The role of career counseling and development professionals was to assist in this process that varied from state to state and from local agency to local agency.

The ***outward extension*** was brought to refocus the nation's educational resources on the very real, difficult scenarios where all students must make it from schooling to jobs.

Finally, an ***inward development*** counseling began for multicultural populations (African Americans, Asian Americans, gays and lesbians, people with disabilities), which resulted in maturing of a profession.

Chapter 18

Indian Perceptions on Counseling

Man is made by his belief. As he believes, so he is

– Bhagavad Gita

Counseling in schools is the bridge that fills the physical, psychological and social needs of the child. School counseling requires a proper recognition and all efforts to be put together to utilize the psychological skill in preventing and in responding to the various psychosocial needs of the school children.

The Indian society with its strong family bonds, a warm community feeling and spiritual essence has been providing the shock absorbers in times of crisis and a support system to deal with the various psychosocial issues. Perhaps, this is one reason for the slow growth of the counseling profession in India.

In the recent years, the Indian society seems to have undergone a total metamorphosis with changing roles of women, a breakdown of the joint family system, increased competitiveness in schools, immense technological advances, peer and parents pressures resulting in stress and strain for the children, where school counselors are like a blessing to the students and to the parents to cope with these situations towards maintaining the mental health of the younger generation.

History of School Counseling in India

School counseling in India is a relatively young profession.

The first Child Guidance Clinic was started by Tata Institute of Social Sciences at Wadia hospital in 1938 and the first school mental health clinic was set up at Nair hospital in 1979. The Ministry of Education, Government of India, established the Central Bureau of Educational and Vocational Guidance in 1954.

After the third five year Plan (1961), guidance services were initiated in schools by the trained counselors and career masters with assistance from school teachers.

By the end of the third five year plan (1966), the number of schools providing guidance service in one form or the other was 3000. But these schools housed only a career master whose job was simply to provide vocational information.

With effect from the year 2000, the Central Bureau of Educational and Vocational Guidance have delegated the work of guidance professionals' training to the Regional institutes of Guidance at Ajmer, Bhopal, Bhubaneswar and Mysore.

Need for Counseling in Schools in India

A big question in the minds of today's educators, policy makers and parents is whether there is a real need for counseling in Indian schools or are we just trying to ape the American norms? Indian society needs to assess whether there really is a room for a professional school counselor. Also, it is important to assess whether the Indian society is ready to accept the services of a counselor or is burdened with stigma towards this service.

In spite these speculations; there is definitely a need for counseling in schools in India. As,

i) There is an evident of increasing number of suicide cases among the school students.

ii) Changing family trends such as working mothers, divorces and single parent families have reduced the emotional cushioning by most of the Indian families.

iii) The immense technological advances, the increased social life and issues such as drug abuse have contributed to stress and strain on the students.

iv) Students undergo,

1. Prolonged feelings of unhappiness, withdrawal, tiredness, lack of interest in daily activities
2. Disturbance in eating or sleeping patterns
3. Difficulties in attention, concentration or memory
4. The feeling of helplessness or overwhelming
5. Sudden shifts in mood or behaviour
6. Increased irritability or suspiciousness towards others
7. Problems in forming and maintaining relationships
8. Difficulties in getting along with peers, family or authority figures
9. Lack of capacity at work
10. State of low confidence or low self-esteem

Counseling leads to,

Academic Success – The school counselors can help the students in realizing their highest potential by removing blocks to academic success, if any.

Personal and Social Development – The school counselor helps to identify talents of the students and helps to nurture these talents by helping them improve their communication and interpersonal skills.

Resolving Psychosocial Problems – Stress, loneliness, bullying, ragging, peer adjustments, parents and teacher pressure are some of the possible psychosocial problems of students that can be resolved by a school counselor.

Counseling for the Teachers and the School Staff

The teachers and the school staff need counseling besides, to deal effectively with the huge number of students with unique individualities coming from diverse backgrounds.

It helps them to,
1. Understand the futility of the Corporal Punishment
2. Feel that each child is unique and accept every student as he/she is
3. Identify learning disabilities of the students
4. Identify psychosocial/adjustment problems of the child
5. Focus on overall development of the students

Chapter 19

Top 20 Principles

*The difference between ordinary and extraordinary is
that little extra*

– Jimmy Johnson

Top 20 Psychological and Educational Aspects of Students Counseling

1. Students Growth Mindset

Students have got the ability to trace their knowledge and intelligence. Few develop a constructive mindset to achieve what they aim or admire at… These may be due to their parents' desires for them, impact by their role models or self-interest upon certain profession. And few students really may not have any such aspirations. It's very important to analyse the student's outlook here. It involves the process of understanding their beliefs on achieving their academic success.

One can curtail their growth, if he or she thinks that just learning the subjects can lead them to success, because it's the false belief they develop. They must be known what real success is and should equip themselves with positivity, disciplined traits, and thirst for continuous update of knowledge.

2. Prior Knowledge

Most of the students nowadays are very proactive in learning things. They learn the subjects in advance which affects their subject knowledge and conceptual growth as well. To make a positive impact out of this, students must be made to go through assessments that bring out their level of subject understandings. Students should be given small projects to execute what they profoundly knew. The rating of these assessments or projects should be discussed with the students to facilitate their conceptual growth and change, which in turn help them to correlate their knowledge they have gained with the subjects.

3. Limits of Stage Theories

Students' intellectualness should not be limited by the general stages of their growth or development. There are cases where even kids possess high IQ's than the elder one and these kids shouldn't be limited saying that they are "just kids" to excel beyond their level and there are so many other such cases where just the age of the person haven't stopped them from doing miracles beyond their accepted standards. Hence, the students mustn't be confined and should be given opportunities based on their learning and growth pace.

4. Facilitating Context of Use

Students' growth and deeper learning are developed, when instructors help them transfer learning from one set of facts to another. Only then, students will be better able to generalize deeper learning, provided, if instructors invest adequate time for them. This skill in students can be developed by using their understanding ability of a particular unit to generate potential solutions for real-world problems.

5. Practice

Acquiring long-term knowledge and skill is highly possible only through practice. This practice has to be initiated by instructors issuing formative assessment frequently through practice problems and sample tests, which help students, increase their knowledge, skills and confidence. Besides, instructors must involve students in practice test activities at spaced intervals to help them achieve greater. Practice tests should include open-ended questions that require both the retrieval of existing knowledge and the challenge of applying that information to new situations or contexts.

6. Feedback

Clear, explanatory and timely feedbacks to students are important for learning. Students have to know their ability and weakness in their subject matters. The marks alone won't let them know how to improve themselves and here is where the role of the teachers is very vital. They should deal with providing feedbacks for the students that makes them to self analyse and work on their strengths' and weaknesses.

A student scoring less mark can decide that he is incapable of studying. But giving him the feedback on where and how he lacked may help him to work on his scopes with better determination. Similarly, a student scoring high marks may limit his learning process thinking that he is done with obtaining knowledge and in this case, he has to be given accurate feedback or remarks to move ahead in his educational ladder.

7. Self-Regulation

Students' self-regulation assists them in better learning and these skills can be taught. It includes being attentive and organized, developing self-control and planning process and memory strategies to improve learning. These skills can be taught through direct instruction and classroom organization.

Teachers can model organizational methods and assist students by focusing on learning targets at the beginning and conclusion of lessons, using classroom calendars, by highlighting difficult concepts that will require more practice, by breaking large projects into manageable components and allowing sufficient processing time through questioning, summarizing and practice.

8. Creativity

Student creativity must be fostered. Creativity is considered as a critical skill for the technology driven world of the 21st century. As it is not a stable trait, it can be taught, nurtured and increased. Creativity can be enhanced using specific methods of structuring assignments and ideas. This can also be done by presenting the students with various situations or problems and involving them to come out with their creative problem solving strategies for those.

9. Motivation

Students gradually tend to enjoy learning when they are intrinsically motivated to understand the importance of learning. Instructors can motivate students through classroom practices and activities that support the fundamental need of students by making them to feel self-reliant. When fed motivation at the right time, the students can understand how their personal abilities can influence their success.

10. Mastery Goals

Students endure the challenging tasks and process information more deeply when they adopt mastery goals rather than performance goals. Mastery goals can be defined as those which are set to achieve supremacy and performance goals are those that satisfy the limited level of success or just end up attempting the tasks. Students who form mastery goals focus on attaining new skills and increase their existing ability whereas students, who develop performance goals, focus simply on showing adequate ability.

When students set performance goals, they have a tendency to avoid tasks that might expose weaknesses and end up missing opportunities that would nurture the development of new skills. Those with mastery goals are more likely to be motivated to learn new skills and achieve higher levels of competence.

11. Teacher Expectations

Teachers' expectations about their students affect the students' opportunities to learn and their learning outcomes. Teachers tend to anticipate students to perform as per their perception on the students which sometimes may mismatch with the students potential. In those cases they need to be flexible in thoroughly examining the students' capacity level and their learning skills.

12. Goal Setting

Setting goals that are short term, specific and moderately challenging enhances growth at ease than establishing goals that are long term, general and overly challenging. Initially, students must be made to set short-term, specific and moderately challenging goals to increase their level of self-efficacy towards building larger goals later. Students should maintain a record of progress toward their ambition which has to be monitored by both the student and the instructor. After students experiencing success with proximal goals, they will be more likely become risk takers, which is one of the most significant attributes to be an achiever of long term goals.

13. Social Contexts

Learning is related with multiple social circumstances. It emphasizes on various communities (families, peer groups, schools, neighbourhoods) of students which they belong to and on how their culture (e.g. shared language, beliefs, values and behavioural norms) influences learning. This is related specifically to the concepts that incorporate culture to increase students' engagement in building stronger relationships with their peers.

14. Interpersonal Relationships

Interpersonal relationships and communication within boundaries can enhance both teaching and learning process and the social development of students. Being too rigid with the students may make them miss their interest towards subjects. Hence, teachers must be flexible or cordial enough in handling the students depending upon their level of response. Communication among the students and with the teachers should be in such a way that, it builds a healthy rapport.

15. Well-Being

Emotional well-being influences educational performance, learning, and development of the students. Self-esteem, self-efficacy, motivation, personality, happiness and coping skills (emotion and stress) are the various components that affect the emotional well-being of the students. These must be well handled both by the teachers (for students) and students (for themselves).

16. Classroom Conduct

Classroom conduct and social interaction are to be learned by the students and can be taught by the teachers through effective classroom instructions on behavioural aspects. Classroom conducts not only shape students' inner personality but also brings them respect for their disciplined traits among the people. One should be inculcated with strong social values and ethics, as without good conducts, gaining knowledge becomes nothing.

17. Expectations and Support

Effective classroom management is based on,
1. Setting and communicating the expectations on students
2. Consistently nurturing positive teacher-students relationships
3. Providing a high level of student support through intrinsic motivation

18. Formative and Summative Assessment

Formative and summative assessments are equally important and useful, but they require different approaches and interpretations. Formative (Minimal level) assessments are typically used as a part of everyday practice and are given either prior to or during instruction. This is conducted to evidence the progress of students' learning in order to provide effective guidance.

Summative assessments, on the other hand, result in an overall evaluation of students' learning or program effectiveness and are typically utilized at the end of a unit or course, thus having more impact on the current instructions. Frequent use of formative assessment accompanied by immediate feedback and specific instruction helps students achieve learning goals and make them assume a greater responsibility towards their own learning process.

19. Assessment Development

Students' skill, knowledge, and ability are best measured with assessment processes grounded with well-defined standards for quality. Formative and summative assessments need to be developed on the basis of student's understanding ability of concepts and not on their ability of just memorizing the subjects. The learning targets of the students must also be considered when preparing the assessments.

20. Assessment Evaluation

Assessment results should display clear, appropriate and fair interpretation of students' knowledge with their subjects. The result of a particular assessment on students learning must be discussed with other educators and the outcomes of discrepancies across the teachers must be monitored. Instructors must be able to accurately interpret test results and clearly communicate the results to students and parents. Descriptive statistics of assessments are more useful for students to examine themselves.

Chapter 20

Counseling is LOVE

Character is doing the right thing, When nobody's looking

–J.C. Wells

At the end of sixteenth chapter, I was saying that, one can doubt, why I narrated my teachers and school life initially, in this context of counseling. I'm breaking up that here…

During 80's there occurred no massive changes in our society. We utilised products made in India. We stayed healthier compared to now. To some extent we led a life of joint family, spent time going cinemas and occasionally visited hotels.

Villages had huts and had default seaters in front of the houses, where people used to relax their time by sharing their problems and get their issues resolved instantly. Getting suggestions (counsel) or advices from the elders and experienced people were at ease those days. Mostly, people were in the state of accepting things light heartedly. We were able to locate trees spreading their branches in dense, covering the space that looked pleasant!

Generally, people had patience and hadn't lost it unnecessarily. They maintained a good rapport with neighbours as like kith and kin. Parents were like parents. Teachers were like teachers. Students were like students. Above all, they were minding their own responsibilities without any anticipation.

Children and students used to play their own discovered games by creating their own toys. They had high level creativity and also had a sound health.

It remained the same at every phase till the end of 90's. Students had no burdens largely and they did not approach studies as a burden either.

Teachers imparted subject knowledge by understanding the potential of the students. Parents supported them at every walks of their life and believed teachers completely. In turn teachers treated students as their own children. There were exceptions too, somewhere here and there.

The troubles started rupturing when these above said scenarios started disrupting!

Chapter 21
Counseling is CARING

– Bhagavad Gita

During my schooling in the village, I was independent and did all that I need, by myself with my maximum involvement. I faced challenges with confidence. There were competitions but not jealousy and when that happened at times, teachers or elders corrected us.

Or else, my parents were there to guide me. To add, I had an intense desire on my life spending each and every day happily. To live such a life wasn't so precious to feel as like now, during those days.

There were no external influences upon me and all these existed only till my eighth grade (i. ebefore joining in hostel).

Everything turned upside down during my ninth to twelfth standard and my life got shrunk inside four walls taking away my liberty. Alike me, most of the students went through the same phase and it was at that point of time, I would had been counseled particularly.

Generally, counseling is meant not only for a particular sphere of people but for everyone. Moreover, every student and equally, every parent must heed that.

This is the reason behind citing me as an example to describe the need of counseling and emphasizing that even a bright student needs counseling at somepoint of time.

Okay! At which phase, I required or one requires counseling, the most?

It's when changing from one school to another or from one environment to another, counseling plays a vital role in helping students to get adapted to those changing situations. For me it's both the school and the environment that had been changed.

Different people, different habits and lifestyle... One had (has) to perform their own duties. Right from cleaning their clothes to cleaning their plates! And I wasn't used to these kinds of habit and its human tendency to get irritated, when we ought to carry out something that we were (are) not used to. Yet, this can be corrected or adapted as days passes.

At some point of time, we need to be the decision maker for ourselves and how to make a decision if we aren't sure whether it's right or wrong?

It hadn't been necessary for me to follow all these when I was in my village... On one fine morning, during holiday, informing my parents that I'm going to play, I left to the mountain with my friends, that was at the visible distance from my place and it had turned dusk by the time I returned home. But nobody panicked asking why I was late and before I was asked, I myself volunteered saying where I went...

It was this mutual trust that built my confidence strong!

But is that possible in hostel life? Only four times a year (Quarterly, Half yearly, Diwali and Pongal seasons) we were allowed to visit our home. Altogether, it was great to have 50 holidays including summer vacations.

But I wasn't able to adapt to that and it was those days where I wandered just as a being with no hope or confidence.

We were allowed to speak with our Father (Mr. Arutthanthai Arulappan) without any restrictions and it was only at that time, I started feeling diffident. But, basically I wasn't so. I was not sure why I pulled myself back in expressing my thoughts to him. This hesitation broke my assurance...

Why didn't I share my mind changes to him? That's a question for which I couldn't find an answer till now. I had spoken with him a lot but hadn't shared my difficulties in those four years even once. The Reason... I do not know!

It's here when I needed counseling or a counselor. There were many other students alike me and each and everyone demanded different method of counseling. Stress, frustration, uncertainty, timidness, over confidence, hesitation, desperateness, lack of confidence and the reason for a counseling to be given to the students can be lengthened...

This is not only the case of hostelites,' but includes the day scholars too... In general, counseling is a common requisite for all the students and genders.

Chapter 22

Counseling is Nothing, But a COMMITMENT

Sever the ignorant doubt in your heart with the sword of self-knowledge. Observe your discipline, Arise

– Bhagavad Gita

For today's generation students, parents and teachers:

"Time is getting changed," is a common ideology prevailing presently. But it'll be fair if we question ourselves whether it's the time that changed(s) or its people who changed(s)?

It can be said that technology has grown rapidly and we have started running behind that…

It's my utmost wish to register my experience in this case as well. Usually, I dislike the habit of hearing or giving advices or to blame or getting blamed and everybody remains so… Right?

I'm the current generation father. My son and daughter are studying sixth and first standard respectively.

I stay little strict with them but when it comes to dance, singing, entertainments I go down to their age and involve myself in those, concurrently. I remain as a friend for them during such times.

But when studies matter, they must be very dedicated and no compromises from my end in that case. If they do not understand any subject matters, I always insist them to keep trying till they infer it and the only advice I give them is, to study only by realising or understanding the subjects...

Besides, I teach them all the possibilities to work out that habit. This is same as what my father said me... I cannot study for them and they have to study for themselves realising their responsibilities.

Yet, my son needs either my wife or me to oversee when he studies or else he eludes from us. But this state is getting changed gradually and he needs nobody beside him if he completely understands his duties.

Not only the subject book he reads, also I have imparted him the habit of reading books that suits his age. Gradually, he himself started reading all kind of comics and thriller books and now, for a long period he has stuck with ghost stories. Guess, he may continue the same for few more days.

One day (it was when he studied fourth standard), he approached me showing a story and said he wrote that. As soon as I read it, I found out that it wasn't his own article and cleared him that if at all he wants to write any stories, he has to write on his own rather imitating others effort.

This happens with elders too... They use to copy it out of their eagerness. The same he had tried. Later, after a long gap, he started writing a series…but this time, it was on his own. I taught him about blogging and he has developed interest towards it.

But his only worry was that nobody appreciated his work and whenever he feels low I use to say him this, "It's not necessary for everyone to read your stuffs. The only task for you is now to write. Just focus on that and after a certain point when you start to pen stories with all your love and interest for it, then undoubtedly everybody will read yours…"

Later, he skipped doing that and started playing games on laptop. When he stays at home, we give him stipulated time to play by slowly cutting down his habit of playing digital games. But whenever we hang out to our hometown, elders and relatives use to pour them with all their fondness which stops us from correcting them those times!

Once, his eyes got swollen by playing video games for hours and from then, he himself stopped spending more time on that. Instead, he started playing outdoor games with his friends.

Children's interests always stay dynamic. It may be due to:
1. Their friends
2. External influences from school
3. Examples cited by their teachers
4. Self influence or impacts by films

And be it anything like these… I use to insist my kids only a thing."Do what you like." But with few conditions,

1. There shouldn't be studies related pending piece of works. Whether its home work or daily school tasks, there should arise no thought like "Let me do it later." If that's the case, then it must be corrected right there.
2. They must perform their duties on their own and when it comes to playing, they should not expect somebody else to sort out their play materials (in maintaining neatness), as it's only them who play.
3. If somebody comes home, they must treat them with respect and should avoid watching television aloud, as it may display a gesture of disrespect for them.
4. If at all they bring their friends to home, they must explain their family values and habits to their friends in advance.
5. They must return home as early as possible if they step out to play and they have to bath compulsorily no matter at what time they enter house after playing.

The above said conditions keep changing its method of execution but not its nature, just like how their thoughts changes…

We are relying on technologies predominantly, nowadays and it's our responsibility to introduce all these techs to our children along with our supervision mandatorily, to get them adapted with the necessary changes.

Also, I ensure to maximum extent that my kids approach their studies just as "A Game."

I wish to move one step ahead and make their studies "A festival" for them and for that we need to mould ourselves perfect. As a first step to that, my wife and I decreased watching television!

The change we felt in the past three years by following this are:

1. We started having food and started sleeping at night at the right time. We got used to additional activity due to this... That's jogging!
2. We made it crystal clear not to dissolve our time in unrelated or unnecessary actions.
3. We are cautious in taking healthy food, when health matters and cooking at home helps us in that case. We go out for lunch or dinner only during unavoidable situations.
4. We hold our control in time management through disciplined activities.
5. My wife started participating in marathon, triathlon which turned possible by our jogging habit.
6. I stay independent and do not restrict anybody. So, I cook myself and send my children to school in the absence of my wife.
7. The next important decision we made is, to set out for various places twice or thrice in a year as a family trip.

The changes we experienced in our kids due to the above routines are:

1. Both of them developed interest for dance and parallely have become health conscious.
2. They step out to play only after completing their homework's.

3. They have become clear about what to watch and what not to watch in television.
4. They also knew their need and selection of stuffs in watching "Youtube."
5. Spending time with relatives and people around, once in a while through excursions have made them to know and think about different kind of people.

We stay as ourselves and have let them to be themselves!

Apart from these, we tend to be edgy and angry at times, which sometimes shows our inability in understanding our kids.

Today's Teachers

When I was young, I used to narrate my parents about my teachers as soon as I reached home and that was due to the impact, my teachers had created on me. Hence, my parents knew about all my teachers.

But, after I joining the hostel, I haven't said them about any of my teachers except Father (Mr. Arutthanthai Arulappan), because he was the one, whom I was closely attached with or it was due to which I stayed in crowd with no uniqueness that led to my timidness which in turn led to my lack of confidence.

It was the government schools that were abundant in those days unlike the current scenario. And now, private schools have bloomed in large numbers. Mostly, it's these institutions and its teachers that impact(ed) students mindset.

Communication has become a very normal action to take place. Google and Youtube come first when someone needs help through which one can self satisfy their needs.

Students' mindset has undergone changes drastically, because of this technological advancements and that has lessen the importance of teachers in their lives. Not only the teachers but almost everybody has lost their importance in their life.

It's because world has been shrunk in their palms through technology. In spite of all these, it's a great achievement, if a teacher is able to impact their students positively and strongly!

Chapter 23

A Letter, Finally!

To the beloved Parents....!

I have got a message to convey you all. Your thought about your kids to grow them as a person of fame by joining them in notable institutions is undoubtedly appreciable. It is certainly right to have bigger dreams for your children to see them pursuing Medicine or Engineering in the renowned colleges or universities!

But remember, these are your dreams for them! Try playing your life along with your children and let them perceive their own dreams and follow their passion to make the game even more interesting or you may end up playing the game alone!

I wish to clear certain things which one may forget or goes unbothered about. Deep think for a minute, before introducing anything to your children or before carrying out any action in front of them...

Question yourself,

1. Whether your dear kid really requires or feels any particular thing very useful that you wish to offer them?

2. Are you discussing with your child before deciding upon anything for them?
3. Is it only you who make decisions for them?
4. Are you letting them to go out and play?
5. Are you making them to socialise with other kids?
6. Are you committing them with responsibilities?
7. Do you want them to understand you, or is that you trying to understand them?
8. Have you ever thought that children are normal humans too?

Assist your children to understand themselves. Explore more about psychological base and its truths. Discuss those with your children.

The more you over impose your child to make them feel happy, the more your child will undergo pressure losing their peace. Hence, do not make them debt their happiness at your own cost!

About
CAREER MUDHRA!

Career Mudhra is a career guidance platform initiated to steer the school students, the graduates and the working professionals in choosing the course of study that fits their interest, in taking up the job that suits their graduation and in deciding the career that matches their acumen respectively.

It promises a counselling session that,

1. Re-discovers one's potential by broadening their vision
2. Changes one's temperament
3. Transforms individuals weaknesses into strengths

Unlike traditional career guidance programs/websites,

Career Mudhra extends high quality career guidance and counseling through unique Career Development Plan at low and affordable cost enabling all the target verticals to get benefitted.

Its Services include,

Training on Career Counseling for,

1. ***Educational Institutions*** – Schools, Colleges and Universities who wish their teachers to be trained on Career Counselling
2. ***Individuals*** who are working as a Teacher, Lecturer, Professor or as an Educator
3. ***Professionals*** who wish to choose Career Counseling as their profession

Psychometric Test for Students and Graduates,

1. Quest

1. It is the test pack for the students of 8th grade to 12th grade.
2. It helps them identify their hidden strengths and thus leads to make smart career decisions.

Test includes,

- Aptitude
- Personality
- Interest
- Skills
- Intelligence

2. Inspirit

1. It is the test pack for the graduates or the students of any stream.
2. It helps them decide the apt career, based on their interest.

Test includes,

- Aptitude
- Personality
- Interest
- Work values
- Intelligence

3. Orbit

This test can be taken by the Engineering Aspirants (Std xi/xii students) to test their interest on various branches of Engineering.

Test includes,

- Aptitude
- Engineering Interest

4. MBA Planner

This test pack is for students aspiring to pursue management students and for the 1st year MBA students.

Test includes,

- Cognitive Test
- Executive skills

5. Collective Cognition

1. This test is created exclusively for the parents.
2. Taking this test helps them to interpret the result with their children's intelligence, skills and learning styles.
3. It also gives the parents, a clear picture to direct their children in choosing their relevant career.

6. Concise

1. It is the test pack for the school students to identify their basic interests.
2. This test helps the students to match their skills with the career pursuit.

Test includes,

- Interest
- Skills

www.careermudhra.com will take you through a short trip to know more about its services and features.

If any queries on Counselling or Career Counselling drop a mail at writersrinivasan@gmail.com srinivasan@careermudhra.com or reach me @ +91–8056010125

Connecting with Career Mudhra makes your present and the future an enlightened one!